GW00497124

il y a des nuac

dans le ci

The Groodoyals of Terre Rouge

by Jude Cowan Montague

Published by
Dark Windows Press
72 Llandudno Road
Rhos-on-Sea
LL28 4EJ
UK

www.darkwindows.co.uk
info@darkwindows.co.uk

Design & layout by Neil Coombs
Printed in the UK

First Edition 2013

0123456789

ISBN-13: 978-0-9571644-8-2

DARK
WINDOWS
PRESS

for Jay & Family

Foreword

De nous koter, maximum ki nou fine fer pou recevoir li, nou fine fer max, dapres nou penser, nou fine recevoir li bien.

Nou fine apprane couma ene etranger pou vivre avec nou. Li ti ena respect la, so simplicity, pas grand noir. Apprecier – kan nou ti celebrer divali, li ti vivre li fully comme ene morisien, p mette deluile p allume la lampe, facon li fer, li ti bien interesser avec seki li ti p fer. Line absorber dan nou culture, li fine rentre dan tous ene tigit. Bien agreable pou nou, avec respect, nou pas ti ena aucune mauvais penser, nou pas ti koner ene camarade aussi proche. Kan zot fine aller, zot fine kit ene vide zot in aller, separer, eloigner, ena sa feeling la ki ene jour pou re joine, zis nou koner ki pou re joine dan lavie. Pas koner si li pou gagne locasion re vini, li most welcome. Mo hope ki kan nou fine recevoir li, line apprecier.

Mo kone li comme chanteuse, mo pas ti koire ki li chante aussi bien. Koter so livre, we are very thankful to you, bien rare nou joine bannes dimounes ki ena bannes penser special, sa montrer line garde ene bon souvenir de nous, mo bien content ki li rappel sa bannes bon souvenir, au nom de toutes la famille, sa initiative ki li fine prend la, li p donne noue ne certaines valeur, a travers so livre. Seki li p share, li true and real in life, sa moment ki li fine vecu, li p ecrire li a atravers so livre, dan ene grand pays comment UK, p reconnaitre nou a travers Jude et so livre.

Our sincere thanks to you and our blessings of success.

Jay Groodoyal
July 2012

Author's Note

For many years my friend Kiran Groodoyal and I had dreamed of a trip to her family home in Mauritius. Backlit pictures of 'La Belle Île' cheered the gloom of the Students' Union offices in East London where we worked together on the university peer support scheme. In November 2007, I booked myself onto a British Airways flight to Port Louis.

Kiran's brothers own a mini-cab business and drove me around the island, showing off its beauty; beaches, waterfalls, religious shrines, and many delightful and sacred locations. I was overwhelmed by the warmth of the welcome and enchanted by the scenery.

One of the first things I did was hunt down a half-decent guitar, and found one in a small music shop in the back streets of Port Louis. Having taken a long sabbatical from song-writing during work on my PhD I was pretty rusty. Influenced by a challenging songwriting course led by Ray Davies I tasked myself to write an album during two weeks. On my last evening after a celebratory biryani I performed the songs and handed on the instrument to the young Groodoyals. The poems came from these ditties and from working on notes and drawings from my sketchbook.

Later, in the printmaking studios at Camberwell School of Arts I developed new pieces from photos, sketches and recollections. Elements of these works have been fragmented and pieced together for this collection.

Acknowledgements

Thanks to Camberwell School of Arts Illustration and Printmaking postgraduate departments for supporting my explorations in etching techniques and experimental drawing.

Thanks for editing support to Helen Mort, Kirsten Irving, Kiran Groodoyal and Andy Jackson and a special thank you to my editor and publisher Neil Coombs.

Grateful acknowledgement is due to the editors of the following journals and anthologies where some of these pieces were first published:

Agnes Meadows at *Loose Muse*; Jenn and Chris at *Extract(s)*; Helen Ivory at *Ink Sweat and Tears*; Thomas Carty at *Carty's Poetry Journal*; Josephine Corcoran at *andotherpoems*; *Writers' Hub* (Birkbeck College, University of London).

Contents

Baie du Tombeau   Arsenal

Grand Baie

PAMPLEMOUSSES

Terre Rouge

Port Louis

moris

île maurice

Map of Mauritius Island

'Mystic Masala'

This is a dark horse parade
into polite lunches on the Port Louis waterfront.

A woman buys a roti and parks her bag
on a white plastic chair, sipping her lassi,
wrapped in the comfort of a walnut brown sari.

I remember that drawing is like riding a bike,
and sketch her ease in fiddling,
her rewinding of cloth,
her throwing of everyday family life
over her shoulder.

I pick up new pencil in burnt umber,
another in cobalt,
bend over backwards to pick up clues,
escaped during the adventure of a crayon line.

Behind the café counter
a dodo crouches.

Terre Rouge i

Mousse, mousse: My job is to wave
this leafy twig to goose flies away.

Jay rolls out sweet potato pills,
we pinch the paste into coconut patties,

Ashna gobbles ice-cream, Dev fries,
shakes the wok, smoke shutters the carport,

The trick is not putting the fire too high.
He scoops out crispy moons.

We cut little wicks for our pottery jars
laid in a swastika on the front drive.

Ash and I hand out freshly cooked sweets
to neighbours, *Namaste, happy Diwali.*

Pour oil in the pots when dark pours down,
light the lamps for missing Sita,

Rama's been fighting for fourteen years,
tonight he'll bring her home .

Morning Walk

Five straggling mongrels
moseyed through a sentence
just to keep a tourist company .
One spotted a frog,
leapt into a ditch
then there were

four disreputable flea-bags
lolling in and out of tongues,
licking the nose of the lost English.
One saw a cicada,
flew barking in the ether
then there were

three motley mutts
answering the foreign nutter
who didn't know her kreol from her lingo.
One smelt a gap,
slipped through in silence.
When she turned she spied

two cheeky curs
running with ruddy conceit
along the red lanes of Arsenal.
One left via the left fork.
which left only one,
the friendliest dog.

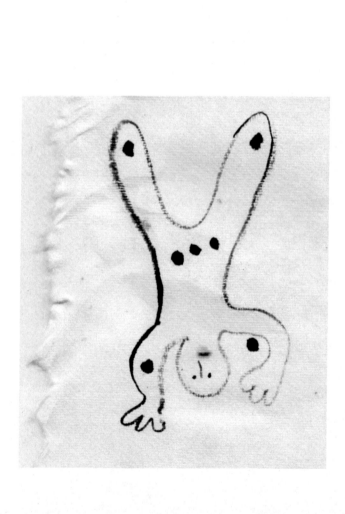

Satee's, Arsenal

If you want her, you will find her *sous les belles étoiles*
Her garden steams in the forest: pomegranate-avocado,

pumpkin-sweet potato. Giant aloes and succulents
become her wild allies. Even the stars pay their respects.

Orion stands on his head for her; and in her parlour,
Micho twitches, dreaming of victory.

Her guests shower in the moonlight, *sous les belles étoiles.*
To receive kindness, stretch up your arms.

Being
Down from t
forest
into my mouth

Pooja

Durga, bring me my love,
out of the river,
tipped in my lap.
Shining silver as an eel in the shallows,
I will snap him when he slips by.

I'm praying, bring me my love,
pulled from deep ocean,
caught with my craft.
If he flash angry as an ancient monster,
let me be the first to tame him.

I glue my *bindi*
and oil my thin arms,
I swirl my *dupatta*.
Kangan jangling, my heart beats louder.
Here in the house of my family
I'm nearly ready, I'm nearly ready.

Durga, bring me my love,
naked from the storm cloud,
rain in my mouth.
If he taste colder than an ice-capped mountain,

my red blood will race to climb him.

I brush my future,
unleash the nightfall,
unbraiding and spilling.

What is coming?

Regarding the sweet potatoes on the wall; *consider the texture*

of their knobbly skin and knowing eyes against the pitted stone;

when a rough boy bounces out, bat ears, brown eyes,

curled teeth, doused in dirt. Shrill screaming sprays gulls

against clouds, and a stallion gallops, frustrated

past plantation machinery. Black nose sniffs for more sound.

One scarlet bird skitters up and away. I run to swing in the banyan tree.

Wiping
table

Washing
Juices

Papayas from the
Family Field at
Illott

L'herbe Sauvage

Jay drove me to the farm
where the family came from.
It wasn't far,
the weather wasn't too grey.

I asked him for papaya.
Reaching some for me
he broke the old tree.

Crossed rows of sugar cane,
(the harvest had finished
so there wasn't much to see)

to a well overgrown with *laliane*,
here his father had drawn water.
Walked on to the stream

saw plastic bags of schoolbooks
dumped. *We swam in the summer,
it was cleaner then.*

*When mother was with us
the crops weren't like this,*
her son stooped to pull
one savage from the soil .

Log

Kiran and I stay in her mother's old home. Like a little wattle and daub Tudor house, it's made from beams from the mountain, and painted white, roofed in corrugated iron sheeting. Her mother and father built this harbour with the oldest children. Dev, second son, carried the longest log.

Last night we went up in the dark to where they had found the wood. That night, there had been a big storm and all the trees had blown down. The government announced that anyone could take them.

The clouds cleared and we beheld the starry archer, bow aimed beyond Port Louis. The children stayed in the minibus, chattering.

The minibus company has grown into a major service with seven buses and four charioteers. Dev and Jay do not drink; not Red Label, not sweet Johnnie Walker. But sometimes they do on Bank Holiday because then NOBODY wants to drive.

Phoenix Beer

Five rupees for the Grande Baie jukebox, please.

41.
ROCK AROUND THE BAY
This guy will have a snack shop.
He can buy you prawns and squid.

85.
SURFIN' MONT CHOISY
He'll be here for the whole week.
It's his boat, he can take you to the coral reef.

115.
CAN'T BUY ME LOVE
His staff have gone home early.
They're taking his money,

32.
BARBARA ANN
they don't want to work.
He's going to sack somebody.

71.
SEE YOU LATER, ALLIGATOR
I didn't realise you were vegetarian.
Oh, you know my uncle?

i ka ha?

(Pamplemousses) is Not the Only Grapefruit

Hallowe'en doesn't scare.
The lotus fountain doesn't work.
Break up the picture and stick it back together
with a bit of Bhojpuri left by grandparents.
She works to make the present
happen with phrases.
I ka ha? What to answer?
I ka ha? I don't know.
I ka ha? Clumps of enormous
undelighypods. A president's garden.
I ka ha? A giant with eyes
of a snake, curled with lashes of vine
trailing long languid leaves.
I ka ha? Lillies on lazy stalks.
Coconut wafers crunch too sweet.
Mosquito ankles swell in the grass.

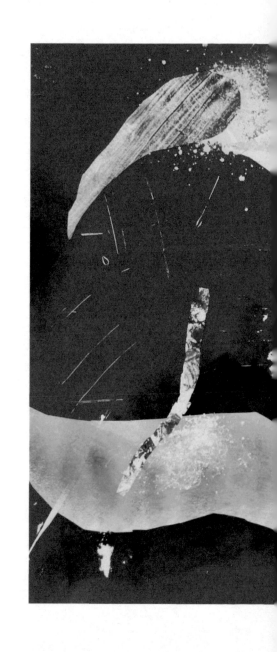

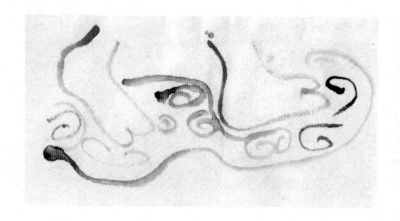

Texting Durga

Toes seek juice
to cool soles on the route

to a small altar
of air-hardened lava.

Where soon for lovers?
Woo her with flowers.

The beach sizzles in cider,
she rides her tiger

showering jewels
on ladies who paddle

oblivious of omens
scratched on beach opals.

Will they drop their Nokias
in wavelets of goddess piss?

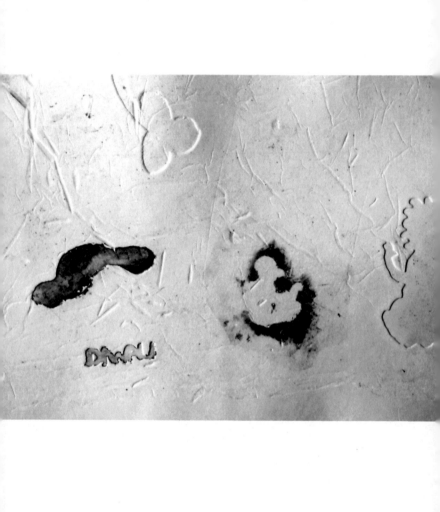

Caterpillars (Baie du Tombeau)

I saved a caterpillar's life,
tipped it on the trunk
where it moved silently upwards.
The bark was rough,
but it climbed hydraulic quick
to find some green.

I think I saved a caterpillar's life,
but being unfamiliar
with the local flora and fauna
I didn't know what it would eat.
Maybe pine is poisonous.

It hauled itself; a moving bridge.
It didn't stop to chew.
Would it have more chance on the trunk
or on the sand?

When I tap a handful of beach onto the tree,
one beast heads up,
one heads down.

Having no papers, being unemployed

The government worker opened the heritage centre especially for Kiran and myself that hot afternoon. These cool, stone cells were where the new indentures would have been held before being taken to their new employers on the sugar plantations. The contract between labourer and employer would have broken down on many occasions and sometimes workers tried to escape with differing degrees of success. From the piled up stocks the government employee gave us a book about vagrancy in nineteenth century Mauritius.

An idler
Incorrigible
A nuisance
Controllable

Sugar prices are falling

Huckstering
Unsanitary
Dirty habits
Convictions

Sugar prices may continue to fall

Grand Port
Grand Riviere
Pamplemousses
Port Louis

Sugar prices may bottom out

Certificate of discharge
Certificate of engagement
Ticket of old immigrant

Sugar prices start rising

Hama Suthoo
Sheik Nunoo
Yasmin Jaomuch
No. 363040

With Major
With Captain
With Mr
With Madame, oh Major, Major, Madame

Malaria bites.
I'm sent back to India
on the Warora.

Belle Mare

Beware bare feet in the war of pine nuts.
Who aims better, who hits harder?
Yu and I pick between coral and starfish.

A fisherman strides over clear pools on tall basalt,
bringing his prisoner, a spike-ball alien
who calls for his starship, mouth mouthing my palm.

Lunging for pirates, loose limbed, Yu swings
monkey-fast up trees, dodges the thrusts
of questions and orders from cousins and aunties.

Treading the sea-fringe, threading
her thoughts through foot-lapping, snaking ripples,
shy Ashna sways as if on a catwalk.

An ice-cream van pipes up Greensleeves, more nasal
than this season's track, Rihanna's 'Umbrella'.
They're getting younger, moans Jay, *While I'm getting older.*

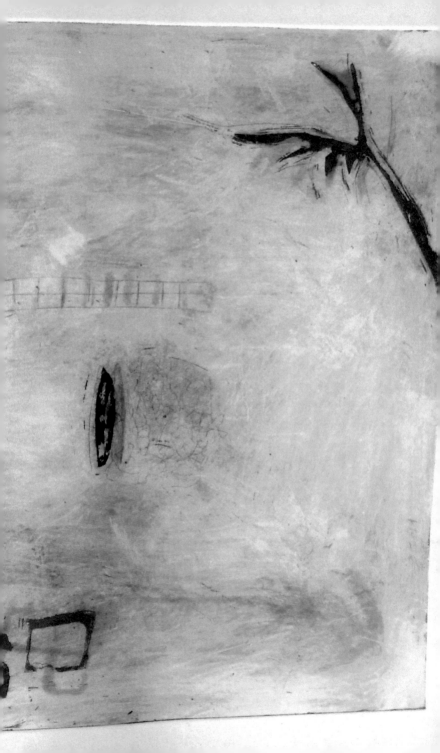

Terre Rouge ii

We climb the breeze blocks
to the top of the roof
to watch the sunset over Port Louis.
Look, we can see the lights of the city
glittering through the trees.
There's a big change coming soon,
Terre Rouge,
the place to be.

We watch the fruit bats
flying overhead, eating jamballac
as they hang from the branches.
Look out over the port,
see the neon of Jumbo
burning through the trees.
And Tianli is coming soon,
it's a big change to
Terre Rouge,
the place to be.

We talk of what has been,
old loves, older dreams,
and stop off in the kitchen,
eating bol renversé.
There's a Hindu soap on the TV
about bigamy,
oh the tears, the tears,
they drip so beautifully.

Balancing on the slope we tell
each other to take care.
I'm straining to see
Capricorn and Sagittarius.
Look out at the stars,
looking down on us whirling round below.
There are big changes coming soon,
Terre Rouge,
the place to be.

Repossession

Houses have crashed to the floor in their old forest home,
blown off their boughs with green needles and tinder pine cones,
a few broken records of last year's young, children long gone.

A yellow bird rebuilds a boudoir from scratch.
She makes little chalets from rubbish, recycling twigs.
Branches catch bedding of kapok, gone seedy, adrift.

A marlin thrashes a lizard's head hard on a rock.
How that poor rubber man swings high and low. He is smashed!
She consumes his innards and shortly her victim has vanished.

Kiran won't swim, it's too late, and her cold isn't done.
I breast stroke quite slowly. She's thinking, sat by the pine.
Wrapped in a towel I patter back over the sand.

Below the horizon, tomorrow and London await us.
Tall shadow-trees take possession of K's special beach.
We step in Dev's van as the sun dives down under the sea.

Illustrations

Names and Glossary

Kiran Groodoyal: My friend and sister

Jay Groodoyal: Kiran's brother

Dev Groodoyal: Kiran's brother

Satee: Kiran's sister

Ashna: Kiran's niece

Yu: Kiran's nephew

Micho: Satee's cat

Bhojpuri: The Groodoyals came from Bihar in eastern India to Mauritius in the nineteenth century, and originally spoke Bhojpuri

Bindi: An ornamental mark worn by a woman on her forehead between her eyebrows, adornment with deep significance

Mousse: Shoo

Namaste: Greeting or salutation originating from India, often accompanied with slight bow and hands pressed together

Diwali: Festival of lights

Dupatta: Scarf

I ka ha: What is that? (Bhojpuri)

Kangan: Bracelet

Mystic Masala: A café on the Port Louis waterfront

Pooja: Worship, adoration

Laliane: A wild plant

Jamballac: A fruit

Bol renversé: Literally 'upside down bowl', a special rice dish

Durga, Rama, Sita: Hindu deities. *Durga* is a fierce, effective goddess who cuts through to the heart of a problem. She rides a tiger.

Pamplemousses, Belle Mare, Port Louis, Arsenal, Terre Rouge, Baie du Tombeau, Grand Baie: Place names

Tianli: A 20 billion rupees industrial project in Riche Terre

Undelighypods: I made this word up

A Dodo's Song

Folky, lively

1. Ve were not special   We were u-nique   They thought we would make a treat   For the crowned heads of Europe

Nine of us were sent to Africa   order Six Genus fifty seven   Nine of us were sent to Africa   ve had our portraits done   Nine of us were sent to Africa   order Six Genus fifty seven   Nine of us were sent to Africa   ve had our portraits done

2. We were not tasty
   We were too tough
   They called us the noxious bird
   But they boiled us up

   One of us was sent to India
   order 6 Genus 57
   To the Mughal Jahangir

3. We grew so decadent
   Forgot how to fly
   Our wings were too weak for our weight
   We had to die

   A skull turned up in Denmark
   Order 6 Genus 57
   Kept in Copenhagen Zoo

4. You've seen me with Alice
   She gave me her prize
   A thimble of fortune
   Futility wise

   Nine of us were sent to Amsterdam
   order 6 Genus 57
   We had our portraits done

71

www.darkwindows.co.uk
info@darkwindows.co.uk

Chili + lemon
from Rodriguez
- you mix up the
whole lemon into
a pulp and mix in
the chili
- I really like it
- there is a green
chili me too
but we only
bought the red

Kiosks conta is getting better 2dy.

Orange with salt is very good for
cold